Palestine Will be Free: Poems on US-Israel Genocide Against the Palestinians

Israel Palestine Conflict Book (What You Need to Know)

Syed Rizvi

DEDICATION

I dedicate this book to the Children of Gaza who were killed by Israeli missiles, the Israeli Army, Israeli oppression, and the Israeli Holocaust.

CONTENTS

BOMBING ON HOSPITAL

In a world scarred by strife and pain,
Where tears fall like the endless rain,
In Oct 2023, a tragedy untold,
A hospital's story, in darkness, unfolds.

Amidst the cries of innocent lives,
Where hope in the shadows quietly survives,
A land occupation and people oppressed,
The anguish of hearts, in sorrow, expressed.

In the heart of a city, where conflict resides,
Gaza hospital stood with humanity's guides,
A sanctuary of healing, compassion's embrace,
Turned into a symbol of a tormented space.

In a moment of chaos, the world held its breath,
As violence descended, sealing their death,
500 souls, in the blink of an eye,
Innocent lives, taken far too high.

For 73 years, a tale of despair,
Injustice and cruelty, the world couldn't bear,
An occupation, a blockade, the cries of the weak,
Innocence lost, as peace seemed so bleak.

Yet, in the darkest of times, there's a glimmer of light,
The world must unite and stand up for what's right,
To end the cycle of pain, to seek common ground,
In the hope that one day, peace will be found.

For love must conquer hatred's cruel grip,
And heal the wounds that conflict may rip,
In Oct 2023, we remember the cost,
Of a world where compassion must never be lost.

OPEN AIR PISON:

In a land where hope should bloom, not wither,
A tale of heartache, a plea to consider,
In the year 2023, Gaza's tears did flow,
As bombs fell from the sky, and darkness did grow.

Westen Media endorsed the Genocide
Innocent souls, their dreams cast aside,
In the rubble and ruins, where children once played,
A story of suffering, humanity betrayed.

A city besieged, its people confined,
An open-air prison, where anguish's entwined,
With hearts that still beat, 'neath the ruins they stand,
A plea for compassion, for a compassionate hand.

For seventy-three years, this tale has been told,
Of occupation's grip, where dreams have grown cold,
Where water and food are used as a chain,
A silent oppression, where sorrow remains.

But let us not forget, in these verses we weave,
The power of unity, the love we believe,
In the hearts of the world, let compassion ascend,
To bring an end to this darkness, to heal and to mend.

Let's stand together, hand in hand,
And rewrite the story of this troubled land,
For peace is the answer, the world must implore,
To end this occupation, to heal and restore.

TALE OF PAIN:

In the shadowed land where sorrows reside,
A tale of pain, where innocence has died,
In Gaza's heart, a truth we can't ignore,
A land besieged, its people crying for more.

For 3785 souls, innocent and pure,
Their dreams and hopes forever obscure,
Innocent lives lost to a relentless war,
Where love, compassion, and peace seem so far.

A relentless cycle, a tormenting stance,
Innocence caught in a tragic circumstance,
A tale of a people oppressed for too long,
Where compassion's silenced, where hearts feel wronged.

Water, food, and aid, a lifeline severed,
A world turning blind to lives that are tethered,
In this endless night, we must kindle a spark,
For peace and justice to make its mark.

The cries of the silenced, the tears in the night,
Must awaken the world, must shine a light,
In the name of humanity, let us take a stand,
To bring an end to this strife-plagued land.

In the name of love, in the name of the free,
May the world unite, may compassion decree,
An end to the suffering, an end to the pain,
In Oct 2023, let peace reign again.

Let's mend the wounds that time can't erase,
And build a world where love takes its place,
For the cycle of violence must meet its end,
In Gaza's heart, let hearts and hands mend.

ISRAEL KILLING BABIES

In the cradle of conflict, where darkness looms,
A tragic tale of children's silenced dreams,
In Gaza's heart, where innocence consumes,
A land ensnared, or so it seems.

Innocence, like fragile petals torn,
1524 children, their futures scorned,
Amidst the chaos, their voices drowned,
Innocence lost, in war's heartless bounds.

Hospitals in ruins, where healing should thrive,
Their cries for help, the world can't deny,
Water, food, and aid, cruelly denied,
Innocent lives, where hope has died.

In the name of justice, we must unite,
To end this darkness, to make things right,
A world divided, compassion denied,
Let's heal the wounds, cast fear aside.

In the face of despair, a call to mend,
For love, not hatred, to be our trend,
The cycle of violence must meet its end,
In Gaza's heart, compassion we must send.

The world must stand, as one hand in hand,
To put an end to the pain-stricken land,
For Allah, God, or the power we confide,
Demands compassion, on either side.

In Oct 2023, let's sow the seeds of peace,
And let the conflict's brutal darkness cease,
Innocence, the guiding star in our stride,
With compassion as our ally, let's cast hate aside.

LITTLE ANGLES

In a world ablaze, where children bear the weight,
Their innocence lost, a cruel twist of fate,
In Gaza's embrace, 1873 angels weep,
Their dreams buried deep in sorrows so steep.

Hospitals reduced to rubble and ash,
Where healing once thrived, now silence in a flash,
A cry for aid, for water and food,
Innocent lives caught in a web so crude.

As darkness prevails and suffering persists,
The world watches on, as pain exists,
Yet, in the hearts of those who still believe,
A yearning for peace, a longing to retrieve.

From the depths of despair, a plea does arise,
To end the war's madness, to dry tear-filled eyes,
United they stand, voices rise as one,
To bring an end to the harm that's been done.

For in the name of love, compassion, and grace,
The world must unite, take up the chase,
To stop the violence, to heal the land,
With open hearts, let us make a stand.

In the name of the innocent, let peace begin,
To break the chains of hatred and sin,
For no god can stand with violence and woe,
It's in our hands, to change, to grow.

Let's cast aside the weapons of despair,
For the power of love, let's fiercely declare,
In Oct 2023, may this world finally see,
The end of suffering, and the dawn of peace, set free.

GAZA'S CHILDERN

In the midst of conflict's thunderous roar,
Where shadows fall, darkening the shore,
Gaza's children, a heartbreaking toll,
Innocent souls, in a world untold.

One thousand five hundred and twenty-four,
Young lives, innocent, forevermore,
Innocence lost to the cruel winds of war,
Their dreams scattered like leaves in a storm.

In the heart of despair, where compassion is rare,
The cries of the innocent fill the air,
Water, food, and aid but a distant prayer,
Hospitals crumble, in this world of despair.

Innocence silenced, their laughter and play,
A world far from innocence, taken away,
In the name of peace, a plea we must send,
To unite as one, let humanity mend.

For the world's gaze must see past the veil,
Of indifference and apathy, we must unveil,
Innocent lives, the price they must not pay,
For wars they didn't start, for strife they didn't weigh.

In the name of love, in the name of the free,
In this world of pain, may compassion decree,
An end to the suffering, an end to the cries,
A world where every child under the same sky flies.

Let us seek a path where peace will ascend,
Where the support of war meets its bitter end,
In the name of unity, may our voices unite,
To stand for the innocent and the right.

For in this world of darkness, hope must reside,
In the hearts of the oppressed, the tears they've cried,
In the name of justice, together we shall stride,
To end the anguish, where innocence has died.

BABIES AND WOMAN

In a world where darkness shrouds the sky,
A tale of sorrow, it's time to clarify,
In Gaza's heart, where tears run deep,
A cycle of violence, we must put to sleep.

Babies and women, lives pure and bright,
Caught in Israeli Bombings, the depths of night,
Innocent souls, their dreams torn asunder,
In a world where compassion, we mustn't blunder.

Hear the cries of Gaza, let hearts open wide,
As destruction and fear swirl like the tide,
A call for humanity to stand hand in hand,
To end the conflict that scars the land.

Water, food, and aid, cruelly cut off,
Innocence silenced, as we stand aloof,
In the name of justice, let's bridge the divide,
With compassion as our ally, together we'll ride.

No one, no one has Allah on their side,
For true faith calls for love as our guide,
In Oct 2023, let's break the chain,
And let peace and compassion once again reign.

In the face of darkness, a glimmer of hope,
Let's find common ground, let's widen the scope,
For love must conquer, let it be our pride,
In Gaza's heart, let's freedom guide.

LIVES IN DESPAIR

In a world gripped by shadows, where sorrow prevails,
A poignant tale of suffering, as the human spirit ails,
In Gaza's heart, where the innocent reside,
A relentless cycle of anguish they can't hide.

Babies, women, civilians, their lives in despair,
Amidst the thunder of bombs, the weight they bear,
Innocence lost, in the chaos, they cry,
As a world watches on, questioning why.

In the name of power, the cries of despair,
A cycle of violence, a world can't repair,
A longing for peace, for love to abide,
In the name of Allah, let compassion be our guide.

For the heavens above, they weep for the lost,
As the tempest of war exacts its cost,
In this tumultuous realm, compassion must preside,
Let's unite for justice, let peace be our stride.

In the name of Allah, or whatever we believe,
Innocence is what we should always retrieve,
In Oct 2023, let's cease the cruel tide,
In Gaza's heart, let compassion reside.

In the realm of humanity, let's bridge the divide,
For no one should stand with darkness on their side,
In unity, we'll find our strength, far and wide,
To end the suffering, freedom can't be denied.

GAZA'S HEART, WHERE SUFFERING RESIDES

In a world where hearts bleed, and tears flow like streams,
A story unfolds, haunting as midnight's dreams,
In Gaza's heart, where suffering resides,
Innocence sacrificed in endless tides.

Babies and women, their voices unheard,
Innocence shattered, like the caged bird,
Amidst the chaos, in the name of pride,
Innocent lives, by violence, denied.

In the wake of destruction, where hope seems to hide,
Innocence lost, like a rising tide,
A cry for compassion, for a ceaseless storm to end,
In the name of love, let hearts transcend.

For no one has Allah, on either side,
To support the horrors where innocence died,
In Oct 2023, let humanity decide,
To end the madness, let compassion be our guide.

The cycle of violence, a darkness profound,
In the name of the innocent, let's turn it around,
For Allah, God, or the power we confide,
Demands compassion and love, to be our guide.

In the face of despair, we must unite,
To heal the wounds, to make things right,
A world divided, let empathy abide,
In Gaza's heart, let freedom be our pride.

ONE SIDE VIEW

In the realm where truth is veiled by shadows deep,
A narrative unfolds, where hearts and secrets weep,
In Gaza's heart, where stories seldom told,
Innocence crushed, while tales of the brave go cold.

A land besieged, where silence reigns supreme,
As civilian lives shatter like a dream,
In the deafening silence, where justice seems denied,
Innocent souls suffer, their voices cast aside.

The media's gaze, a one-sided view,
Where only one narrative breaks through,
Innocence, like forgotten whispers in the night,
Invisible, unheard, robbed of their light.

In the midst of darkness, a call for change,
To shift the lens, a perspective rearrange,
For every life deserves its story's grace,
A chance to be heard, to take its place.

In the name of truth, let voices rise,
To unveil the pain behind the veiled skies,
For in unity, compassion, and light,
We can rewrite the narrative, make it right.

In Oct 2023, let's tear down the divide,
And in the name of justice, let humanity's flag fly high,
For Gaza's heart, with its stories untold,
Deserves its rightful place in history's fold.

LOOK THE OTHER SIDE

In a world of shadows, where truth is concealed,
A tale of suffering, too long to be healed,
In Gaza's heart, where lives are torn,
A story untold, of those who mourn.

Civilians caught in the relentless storm,
Their stories neglected, their voices forlorn,
While media's gaze on the occupier's side,
The silenced suffering, the truth denied.

The innocent souls, in the crossfire they stand,
Their plight unseen, by the world's grandstand,
In a narrative skewed, where justice is veiled,
Their tears and their pain forever unveiled.

A media's lens, a distorted view,
A tale of oppression, forever askew,
But beyond the headlines, the bias, the spin,
In the name of justice, let us begin.

To lift the voices that long to be heard,
To honor the silenced, their pain undeserved,
For empathy transcends the boundaries we find,
In the hearts of the many, a compassionate bind.

In Oct 2023, let truth unfurl its wings,
Let compassion reign, as empathy sings,
A world where all stories find their place,
And justice and love take their rightful space.

THEY CAN'T HIDE

In a world where voices should be free,
A tale of silenced truth, let us all see,
In Gaza's heart, where courage abides,
A land oppressed, where justice hides.

Beneath the weight of countless tears,
A tale of struggle through endless years,
Invisible stories of the oppressed untold,
Innocent lives, in shadows, they fold.

While bombs rain down on homes and streets,
Media bias masks the heart's true beats,
Focusing solely on the oppressor's view,
The silenced voices remain but a few.

Amid the chaos, where compassion's denied,
The suffering masses, they can't hide,
Innocent lives caught in a cruel divide,
In a world where truth's been cast aside.

But let us seek the hidden, the untold,
In Oct 2023, may the world behold,
The silenced truth, the pain that resides,
In Gaza's heart, where hope yet abides.

The media's role, to expose, not to shield,
Let impartiality be the truest shield,
For in the face of oppression, let truth decide,
The story untold, compassion be our guide.

In the name of justice, let voices be freed,
For every soul in need, every heart that bleeds,
May the world unite, in truth's embrace,
To reveal the hidden stories, to heal and find grace.

MEDIA INTERVIEW

In a world where shadows cling to whispered fears,
A tale unfolds, heavy with unspoken tears,
In Gaza's heart, where innocent lives collide,
A stark reality, where truth refuses to hide.

Beneath the endless sky, where hope seems frail,
Civilians, by violence, caught in a sorrowful trail,
Innocence stripped, their cries in the wind,
Their silent voices, the world must rescind.

An interview, a revelation in the air,
An Israeli soldier's words, a truth laid bare,
Admitting to a war against the innocent's hold,
A revelation that shakes the story we've been told.

In the name of justice, let's break the divide,
And let empathy and truth forever coincide,
For Gaza's heart deserves its place in the light,
In Oct 2023, let's steer the world right.

To mend the wounds, we must unite,
Shatter the veil, let compassion ignite,
A world where innocence shall not be denied,
In Gaza's heart, let peace be our guide.

CNN NEWS INTERVIEW

In the echoes of conflict, where darkness prevails,
A harrowing story, a heartrending tale,
In Gaza's heart, where innocent souls roam,
Innocence besieged, a land turned to stone.

With every bomb's explosion, a life's flickering flame,
Civilian hearts caught in this merciless game,
In the midst of despair, a truth revealed,
An interview's confession, the hidden sealed.

The CNN stage, a moment of reckoning,
A soldier's admission, the world's collective questioning,
A war against civilians, stark in the light,
A truth too painful to endure, to be right.

In the name of justice, let compassion guide,
The stories untold, on either side,
In Oct 2023, may empathy be our creed,
To heal the wounds, where innocence must be freed.

The cycle of violence, let it now unwind,
For in unity and love, new hope we shall find,
In Gaza's heart, where stories unfold,
Let humanity's compassion be the story retold.

SAVE THE BABIES IN GAZA

In Gaza's heart, where innocence dwells,
A dire plea amid war's dreadful knells,
Babies crying, their voices in the night,
Amidst the chaos, seeking the light.

Innocence besieged, by violence confined,
The world must unite, with hearts aligned,
To save these babies, so pure and small,
From terror's grip, let love be our call.

In the shadow of conflict, let compassion rise,
As tears fall from innocent eyes,
For in their innocence, hope takes root,
Let's shield these babies from the path of brute.

The cries for help, in the darkest hour,
Are a testament to a world's collective power,
In Oct 2023, let's find a way,
To save these babies, come what may.

For in the name of love, compassion, and grace,
We'll stand together to protect their fragile space,
In Gaza's heart, let our humanity bloom,
And rescue these babies from a life of gloom.

ISRAEL KILLING BABIES IN GAZA

In the cradle of conflict, where innocence cries,
Babies in Gaza beneath the dark skies,
They are the hope, the dawn's tender light,
Caught in the crossfire, a perilous fight.

Tiny hearts, untouched by the world's strife,
Innocence incarnate, the essence of life,
Their cries for salvation, a desperate plea,
To save them from terror, to set them free.

In the name of humanity, let's unite as one,
To shield these young lives from what's done,
For in the eyes of a child, pure and wide,
Lies the future we must protect, side by side.

Let's end the cycle, break the chain,
No more tears, no more innocent pain,
In Oct 2023, let's rise above,
To save these babies, let there be love.

In the name of compassion, let courage guide,
To shelter these angels, no need to hide,
For the world must stand, no more despair,
To keep these babies safe, in love's tender care.

DESPERATE CRIES

In the heart of a struggle, where tears fill the skies,
A plea for the innocent, their desperate cries,
In Gaza's embrace, where babies reside,
Innocence seeks refuge, hope alongside.

Tiny souls, like stars in a moonless night,
Their laughter stolen, their dreams out of sight,
Innocence in peril, in the turmoil they're stuck,
Their world filled with terror, their lives run amok.

Innocence, like blossoms in fields torn asunder,
Innocence, a treasure, humanity's wonder,
Let's shield them from harm, let compassion unite,
In the face of darkness, let love be the light.

For the world must stand, hand in hand,
To protect the helpless, to take a firm stand,
Against the storm of conflict, the shadow of despair,
In Gaza's heart, let humanity repair.

In Oct 2023, let love be our creed,
To rescue the babies from the terror they heed,
From Israeli bombings, from fear's cruel ruse,
May innocence triumph, may they find their muse.

In the name of hope, let's break down the wall,
A world without violence, where love stands tall,
Let the babies of Gaza know they're not alone,
In a world filled with compassion, their hearts will be home.

SAVE INFANTS IN GAZA

In the cradle of strife, a tale we unveil,
Of babes in Gaza, where courage prevails,
Israel's bombings, a relentless crusade,
Innocence besieged in shadows they fade.

With tears in their eyes and hearts filled with fear,
These children, in anguish, their voices unclear,
With nowhere to run, no safe harbor found,
Their cries for salvation in echoes resound.

Amidst the destruction, they yearn for the light,
For aid to reach them, dispel endless night,
In the face of adversity, they stand brave,
Through darkness and chaos, their spirits they save.

The world must unite, their cause to defend,
In the name of compassion, let hate meet its end,
In October of 2023, let love lead the way,
To rescue these children from fear's fierce array.

In epic poetry's embrace, we shall impart,
The valor of these young souls, a tale from the heart,
May they find their salvation in humanity's grace,
And from the cruel tempest, find a safer place.

GAZA'S HEART

In Gaza's heart, where sorrow's tempests brew,
A tale unfolds, of infants pure and true,
To save these babes from bombs and terror's might,
Their desperate cries pierce through the darkest night.

Innocence, beset by war's cruel hand,
Within a tumult, where fear takes its stand,
No refuge found, no sanctuary near,
Young lives adrift, in chaos and in fear.

The world must rise, as one united soul,
To halt the storm, to heal and make them whole,
In October of 2023, let peace ascend,
To shield these babes and make the nightmare end.

In epic verse, their stories shall be told,
Of courage, love, and hearts both brave and bold,
Innocence, in unity, shall find its way,
As hope and empathy light up their day.

CRY FOR HELP

To save the babes of Gaza, midst the fray,
From Israel's ceaseless storms and terror's sway,
Young voices cry for help, lost in despair,
With nowhere left to turn, they need our care.

Innocence in turmoil, in shadows stands,
Amidst the chaos, in these war-torn lands,
No refuge left, no haven to be found,
Innocent lives, on fragile ground.

The world must rise, with empathy and might,
To shield the children from the endless night,
In October of 2023, let kindness steer,
To halt this cycle of relentless fear.

May love and peace unite to pave the way,
To guide these babes to brighter, safer days,
Innocence, in unity, shall find its grace,
As compassion's light shall lead the human race.

SAVE THE NEW BORNS IN PALESTINE

To save the babes in Gaza, midst the storm,
From Israel's bombings, terror's cruel norm,
Their cries, like whispers in the darkest night,
No refuge found in the chaos and the fight.

Innocence, besieged, their futures hung askew,
As violence rages, their hopes are far and few,
With desperate pleas for aid, they wait in dread,
No sanctuary found, as tears are shed.

The world must hear their desperate cries,
To shield these children from relentless skies,
In Oct 2023, let's stand as one,
To end this pain, to see the rising sun.

With love and peace, let's bridge the great divide,
And in compassion's name, let hearts be our guide,
To save the babes in Gaza from their plight,
To turn the darkness into hopeful light.

YOUNG BABES IN GAZA

To save young babes in Gaza's heart of plight,
From Israel's ruthless bombs and terror's blight,
Their cries of anguish pierce the heavy air,
No refuge found, no solace anywhere.

Innocence, in shadows, trembling in despair,
As war's relentless flames consume the air,
Their plea for aid, unanswered in the night,
In the midst of chaos, no glimmer of light.

The world must stand, their voices to defend,
To shield the children from a tragic end,
In Oct of 2023, let compassion sway,
To bring an end to this relentless fray.

May peace and love, in unity, emerge,
To mend the hearts, these innocent souls to purge.

INFANTS IN GAZA

To save the infants in Gaza's dire plight,
From Israel's bombs and terror's relentless might,
The children's cries pierce through the shattered air,
With nowhere to seek refuge, no one seems to care.

Innocence at stake, in this relentless fight,
No aid can reach them in the dark of night,
The world must wake to their heart-wrenching plea,
And end the daily bombings, let these young ones be.

In Oct 2023, let compassion bloom,
To shield the babes from this relentless gloom,
With love and peace, we'll mend what's torn apart,
And heal the wounded innocence, let it restart.

ISRAEL'S BOMBINGS, CIVILIANS

To save sweet babes in Gaza's throes of woe,
From Israel's bombings, terror's cruel embrace,
Their tiny hearts cry out, where'er they go,
No refuge found in this heart-rending space.

Innocence weeps, a world turned cold and gray,
In the shadowed veil of endless strife,
For little ones, no haven on this day,
No aid to reach them in this bitter life.

The world must heed this desperate, anguished plea,
As Israel's bombings haunt each passing sun,
Let love and peace restore humanity,
To shield these babes, their battles yet unwon.

In Oct of 2023, let kindness rise,
To save these children from tear-filled skies.

A PLEA FOR PEACE

In Gaza's heart, where innocence doth weep,
Babies' cries, like the tears of heavens vast,
From Israel's bombs, their slumbers interrupt,
A plea for peace, a future unsurpassed.

Innocence trapped, in turmoil's cruel embrace,
No refuge found, in terror's endless tide,
Innocent babes, their dreams displaced,
In war's cruel shadow, where angels hide.

With aid denied, their voices strained in prayer,
They long for solace, for a safer shore,
In Gaza's heart, a world ensnared,
Innocence suffers, the pain we can't ignore.

In Oct of Twenty-Twenty Three, let's vow,
To shield these babes, to wipe their tear-stained brow.

BABIES IN GAZA BENEATH THE DARK SKIES

In the genocide, humanity cries,
Babies in Gaza beneath the dark skies,
They are the hope, the dawn's tender light,
Caught in the crossfire, a perilous fight.

Tiny hearts, untouched by the world's strife,
Innocence incarnate, the essence of life,
Their cries for salvation, a desperate plea,
To save them from terror, to set them free.

In the name of humanity, let's unite as one,
To shield these young lives from what's done,
For in the eyes of a child, pure and wide,
Lies the future we must protect, side by side.

Let's end the cycle, break the chain,
No more tears, no more innocent pain,
In Oct 2023, let's rise above,
To save these babies, let there be love.

In the name of compassion, let courage guide,
To shelter these angels, no need to hide,
For the world must stand, no more despair,
To keep these babies safe, in love's tender care.

GAZA DIRE PLEA

In Gaza's heart, where suffering dwells,
A dire plea amid war's dreadful knells,
Babies crying, their voices in the night,
Amidst the chaos, seeking the light.

Innocence besieged, by violence confined,
The world must unite, with hearts aligned,
To save these babies, so pure and small,
From terror's grip, let love be our call.

In the shadow of conflict, let compassion rise,
As tears fall from innocent eyes,
For in their innocence, hope takes root,
Let's shield these babies from the path of brute.

The cries for help, in the darkest hour,
Are a testament to a world's collective power,
In Gaza holocaust, let's find a way,
To save these babies, come what may.

For in the name of love, compassion, and grace,
We'll stand together to protect their fragile space,
In Gaza's heart, let our humanity bloom,
And rescue these babies from a life of gloom.

MEDIA AND WEST

In a world where truth should brightly shine,
There's a darkness where our hopes decline,
As media and West, with blinkered eyes,
Support the unjust, where innocence dies.

In Gaza's heart, where courage resides,
A tale of struggle, the pain it hides,
Yet headlines twist and turn the tale,
As if the cries of Gaza will ever fail.

For justice should be blind, but can it see,
The suffering in Gaza, humanity's plea?
Where people's lives are deemed so small,
A world divided, compassion's call.

Innocence is lost amidst the fray,
As narratives shift in a twisted way,
In Oct 2023, we must unite,
To shed the bias, to shine the light.

For every life holds a sacred flame,
And no one's suffering should be fair game,
In Gaza's heart, let empathy swell,
A world together, in unity, we shall.

So, let's rewrite the narrative, make it clear,
That compassion and truth are what we hold dear,
For in the name of humanity, we stand,
To create a world where justice will expand.

STORIES OFTEN TWIST AND TURN

In a world where stories often twist and turn,
Let me shed some light on what's discerned,
In a spoken word, these truths I'll lay,
About the darkness we must face today.

How media and the West, a dance they choreograph,
Supporting Israel, their unwavering staff,
For war crimes and terrorism, they turn a blind eye,
Innocent lives in Gaza, they let them die.

The headlines paint a skewed tale, it's clear,
But let's dig deeper, let's cast off our fear,
In Gaza, where every life should hold sway,
Why do we let these horrors have their way?

People's lives in Gaza, do they not matter?
Or is humanity's conscience lost in the chatter?
Innocence lost to the noise of war's rattle,
Yet the world keeps silent, as if in a battle.

But in the face of this darkness, we'll take a stand,
Hand in hand, we'll rewrite the plan,
For humanity, for Gaza, we'll make it right,
And let compassion guide us, through day and night.

No more shall silence be our demise,
The truth unveiled, no more disguise,
In this spoken word, we'll let justice unfurl,
For Gaza's people, for every boy and girl.

SUPPORTER OF HOLOCAUST

In the pages of history, a shadow we must face,
A solemn truth we can't afford to erase,
The Holocaust's horrors, we remember them well,
Innocence lost in a nightmarish spell.

But now, a new chapter, a story untold,
Where inhumanity's tale continues to unfold,
In Israel's actions, some see shades of the past,
A painful comparison that we must cast.

If you weep for the Holocaust, for its victims' despair,
Can you then, in good conscience, ignore and not care?
For crimes against humanity, we must take a stance,
In the name of justice, we'll raise our voice and advance.

For no suffering should be diminished or weighed,
In the balance of justice, we'll stand unafraid,
In the echoes of history, we'll find our way,
To ensure that love and compassion hold sway.

In the face of oppression, we'll be the guide,
A new narrative where humanity will not hide,
For history's lessons, we'll heed their call,
In this spoken word, justice shall enthrall.

GAZA HOLOCAUST

In a world of pain and history's tears,
Let's confront the shadows, face our fears,
For if we cry for the Holocaust's dark stain,
We cannot support oppression's cruel reign.

A history etched in suffering and despair,
The Holocaust's horrors, we must be aware,
But how can we stand for justice and truth,
If we close our eyes to oppression's uncouth?

For Israeli actions, like a page from the past,
Echo with questions, they cannot outlast,
In the name of humanity, let's take a stand,
And say, "Never again" to oppression's cruel hand.

It's not about sides or who's right or wrong,
But the cry for justice must be strong,
In the face of cruelty, let's unite,
To ensure every soul sees the light.

For history's lessons, let's not forget,
The pain and suffering, the lasting regret,
If we cry for the Holocaust's heart-wrenching times,
Then oppression's darkness, we must redefine.

THE HOLOCAUST'S PAIN

In the echoes of history, a somber refrain,
The Holocaust's pain, forever ingrained,
A lesson we must heed, a memory we hold,
For the depth of human suffering, stories untold.

But in this complex world, where shadows loom,
We must discern the truth, in every gloom,
To cry for the Holocaust, the past's darkest side,
Demands we stand for justice, far and wide.

Yet, the present's tale, a moral divide,
When innocent lives in Gaza subside,
To support Israeli actions, we must beware,
For humanity's values, we must declare.

To label it "Nazi-like" or worse, we must be just,
In our pursuit of truth, in whom we trust,
Let history guide us, with lessons to confide,
In the name of justice, let compassion be our guide.

In this spoken word, let's break the silence's chains,
Seek empathy, justice, as our conscience remains,
For the cries of the oppressed, we cannot ignore,
In the name of humanity, let justice restore.

CRIMES AGAINST HUMANITY

In the heart of Gaza, where innocence resides,
A tragedy unfolds, where the truth abides,
Kids fall victim to Israeli bombs of hate,
Innocence lost, sealing a tragic fate.

Amid the rubble, where their dreams once soared,
Innocent children, their futures ignored,
The world bears witness to this cruel calamity,
As lives are shattered by relentless enmity.

In the halls of power, where decisions are made,
A veto casts shadows, in the darkness it's laid,
To stop the genocide, we plead for the right,
For humanity's sake, let justice take flight.

For the memories of these young souls shall endure,
In the annals of time, their stories pure,
The world's conscience shall bear the weight,
Of lives lost too soon, in this cruel twist of fate.

In this spoken word, let's unite, let's proclaim,
That justice and peace should be our aim,
For the children of Gaza, let us stand as one,
Their memory shall shine, like the morning sun.

The veto that silenced cries in the night,
Shall be remembered as a blemish, not right,
A crime against humanity, we shall not forget,
As we strive for a world where no child's tears are met.

ISRAELI BOMBS RAINING

In the heart of Gaza, where innocence resides,
Kids fall victim to the tumultuous tides,
Israeli bombs raining, the sky's bitter tear,
Innocence lost, in the name of fear.

In the halls of power, where decisions are made,
A veto is cast, in the darkness it's laid,
A crime against humanity, a silence profound,
In the name of justice, let the truth resound.

For kids are our future, our hopes and our dreams,
Innocent lives torn at the very seams,
In Gaza's heart, let their memory prevail,
Their stories, their laughter, we will not curtail.

In the annals of history, let it be known,
A world that stood silent, hearts turned to stone,
But in our remembrance, their legacy will shine,
Innocence lost, their memory enshrined.

May their sacrifice ignite a world to unite,
For the sake of humanity, in the name of what's right,
In this spoken word, let compassion guide our way,
To stop the genocide, to see a brighter day.

BOMBS SHATTER DREAMS

In Gaza's heart, where innocence should thrive,
Bombs shatter dreams, as young lives strive,
Kids, their laughter silenced in the night,
Innocence lost to war's relentless might.

As the world looks on, a veto stands tall,
USA's choice, to answer the call,
To stop the genocide, or let it proceed,
A moment in history, where hearts still bleed.

For kids who perished, in a world so unjust,
Their memory etched in history's trust,
Innocence, a casualty in the strife,
A crime against humanity, a stain on life.

In the spoken word, let their stories resound,
Their names, their hopes, in our hearts are found,
In the name of justice, let's rewrite the decree,
And ensure that in their memory, we set innocence free.

BIDEN'S SUPPORT FOR WAR CRIMES

Biden, I raise my voice, make it clear,
Your actions in Gaza, we hold dear,
A support for war crimes, it can't be denied,
Innocent lives crushed, in darkness, they hide.

Your veto in the UN, a deafening silence,
While Gaza's heart aches in relentless violence,
For the world watches on, as children fall,
Innocence sacrificed, like a whispered call.

In this spoken word, let the truth be heard,
A leader's actions, in the court of the world,
For war crimes and justice, we must unite,
In the name of humanity, we demand what's right.

Biden, the choice is yours, the power to decide,
To stand for the truth, or let innocence subside,
In the name of peace, let justice be sown,
For Gaza's children, they can't bear this alone.

BIDEN, OH BIDEN

Biden, oh Biden, hear our voice resound,
A choice to make, on what moral ground,
Support for Gaza's war crimes, a shadow cast,
Your veto at the UN, a moment that will last.

Innocent lives, in the darkness, they stand,
Their cries for justice, a plea to the land,
But your stance, it leaves us torn,
A verdict on humanity, a promise worn.

We long for a leader with compassion in sight,
To stand for what's just, to do what is right,
In this spoken word, we raise our plea,
For Gaza's suffering, for humanity to be free.

In the ballot box, we'll make our stand,
For justice, for peace, across the land,
The power to change, to make amends,
For in unity, a brighter future descends.

GENOCIDE CALL

In the realm of airwaves, a toxic tale unfurls,
Where hate is sown, where the rhetoric swirls,
Conservative talk radio, a platform of might,
Spreading venomous words, in the absence of light.

Vicious and anti-Palestinian, the language they choose,
In recent days, it's a message we must refuse,
For in the power of words, there's a world at stake,
When hate is fueled, the ground begins to quake.

Linzy Gram's words, a dangerous decree,
"Level Gaza," he says, with a heart so free,
Dehumanizing rhetoric, genocidal call,
That incites terror and makes compassion fall.

In this spoken word, let's reject the hate's tide,
For words have power, where humanity resides,
In unity and empathy, let's find our way,
To heal the wounds and usher in a brighter day.

CONSERVATIVE TALK RADIO

In the realm of airwaves, voices take their stand,
A rhetoric so fierce, sweeping o'er the land,
Conservative talk radio, a platform, they employ,
But the words they wield, we must all be coy.

For in the echo chambers, hatred breeds,
As the seeds of division, it sows and feeds,
Lindsey Graham's words, like a fiery storm,
A dehumanizing rhetoric, a dangerous norm.

Such genocidal whispers, in the air they linger,
Inciting fear, pointing fingers,
Against Palestinians, Muslims too,
In the name of peace, what can we do?

In the spoken word, let the truth resound,
Hatred's chains, we must unbound,
For unity and love, let's take the lead,
To plant compassion's seed, let's be the change we need.

WHY TURN A BLIND EYE

In a world of questions, we must inquire,
Why turn a blind eye, let justice transpire,
Supporting actions that mirror history's stain,
In Gaza's heart, where innocent lives are slain.

To label it as such, a solemn cry,
Like Hitler's crimes, where millions did die,
Innocence in Gaza, in darkness, they tread,
As the world watches on, what's left unsaid.

For truth in spoken word, let's pave the way,
A voice against injustice, in the light of day,
To stop this cycle of pain and despair,
In the name of humanity, we must be aware.

In the echoes of history, let's rewrite the scene,
For Gaza's people, let empathy convene,
In the face of silence, let courage guide,
To end the suffering, to heal the divide.

WHITE PHOSPHORUS FALLS

In the cradle of conflict, where darkness takes hold,
White phosphorus falls, a story unfolds,
A war crime committed, it's clear as day,
Human suffering, where innocence may sway.

Babies, women, children, their lives in the fray,
As white phosphorus descends, in the darkest display,
Innocent civilians caught in its flame,
A cruel, burning sorrow, we must name.

In the spoken word, let the truth ignite,
Expose the horrors hidden from sight,
For in Gaza's heart, where suffering resides,
Humanity's conscience, we can't let it hide.

Let's stand as one, let compassion ignite,
To end the suffering, in day and night,
In the name of justice, let the world unite,
For Gaza's people, let's set things right.

www.ingramcontent.com/pod-product-compliance
Lightning Source LLC
Chambersburg PA
CBHW081242020426
42331CB00013B/3269